26 a

P9-CWD-610

DATE DUE	

WORLD ALMANAC® LIBRARY OF THE STATES

Pennsylvania

THE KEYSTONE STATE

by Scott Ingram

Curriculum Consultant: Jean Craven,
Director of Instructional Support,
Albuquerque, NM, Public Schools

WORLD ALMANAC® LIBRARY

974.8
I

Please visit our web site at: www.worldalmanaclibrary.com
For a free color catalog describing World Almanac® Library's list of high-quality books and multimedia programs, call 1-800-848-2928 or fax your request to (414) 332-3567.

Library of Congress Cataloging-in-Publication Data

Ingram, Scott (William Scott).
    Pennsylvania, the Keystone State / by Scott Ingram.
        p. cm. — (World Almanac Library of the states)
    Includes bibliographical references and index.
    Summary: Illustrations and text present the history, geography, people, politics and government, economy, and social life and customs of Pennsylvania, which boasted the first hospital in the United States.
    ISBN 0-8368-5120-X (lib. bdg.)
    ISBN 0-8368-5291-5 (softcover)
    1. Pennsylvania—Juvenile literature. [1. Pennsylvania.] I. Title. II. Series.
F149.3.I58 2002
974.8—dc21   2001046985

This edition first published in 2002 by
World Almanac® Library
330 West Olive Street, Suite 100
Milwaukee, WI 53212 USA

This edition © 2002 by World Almanac® Library.

Design and Editorial: Jack&Bill/Bill SMITH STUDIO Inc.
Editors: Jackie Ball and Kristen Behrens
Art Directors: Ron Leighton and Jeffrey Rutzky
Photo Research and Buying: Christie Silver and Sean Livingstone
Design and Production: Maureen O'Connor and Jeffrey Rutzky
World Almanac® Library Editors: Patricia Lantier, Amy Stone, Valerie J. Weber, Catherine Gardner, Carolyn Kott Washburne, Alan Wachtel, Monica Rausch
World Almanac® Library Production: Scott M. Krall, Eva Erato-Rudek, Tammy Gruenewald

Photo credits: p. 5 © PhotoDisc; p. 6 (all) © Corel; p. 7 (clockwise) © Corel, © Hershey, © Corel, © ArtToday; p. 9 © Corel; p. 10 © Corel; p. 11 © ArtToday; p. 12 © Francis G. Mayer/CORBIS; p. 13 © ArtToday; p. 14 © Corel; p. 15 © Bill Pierce/TimePix; p. 17 © Corel; p. 18 © PhotoDisc; p.19 © Painet; p. 20 (from left to right) © Corel, courtesy of Berks County CVB, courtesy of Bucks County CVB; p. 21 (from left to right) courtesy of Bucks County CVB, courtesy of Pocono Mountain Vacation Bureau, courtesy of Hickory Run State Park; p. 23 © Corel; p. 26 (all) © PhotoDisc; p. 27 courtesy of Martin Guitar; p. 29 © Richard T. Nowitz/Corbis; p. 30 © Win McNamee/TimePix; p. 31 © Library of Congress; p. 32 © Corel; p. 33 (from left to right) © ArtToday, © Corel; p. 34 (left) © Corel, (right) © PhotoDisc; p. 35 © Richard A. Cooke/Corbis; p. 36 © Jason Cohn/TimePix; p. 37 courtesy of Hickory Run State Park; p. 38 (all) © ArtToday; p. 39 © PhotoDisc; p. 40 © Reuters/TimePix; p. 41 © Fred Prouser/TimePix; p. 42 © Library of Congress; p. 44 (clockwise) © PhotoDisc, © Artville, © ArtToday; p. 45 © Corel

Printed in the United States of America

1 2 3 4 5 6 7 8 9 06 05 04 03 02

Pennsylvania

INTRODUCTION	4
ALMANAC	6
HISTORY	8
THE PEOPLE	16
THE LAND	20
ECONOMY & COMMERCE	24
POLITICS & GOVERNMENT	28
CULTURE & LIFESTYLE	32
NOTABLE PEOPLE	38
TIME LINE	42
STATE EVENTS & ATTRACTIONS	44
MORE ABOUT PENNSYLVANIA	46
INDEX	47

Turning the Key

Turn a map of the United States sideways, so the Atlantic Coast faces south, and you can see why Pennsylvania is called the Keystone State. In an archway the keystone supports the weight of the other stones pressing against it from either side. In the early history of our nation, Pennsylvania lay exactly between the industrial northern states and the agricultural southern states. The pressure of turning thirteen separate colonies into one nation was brought to bear on Pennsylvania's largest city, Philadelphia. It was there that the United States was created.

Pennsylvania, from its very beginning, truly embodied the best U.S. principles — a colony that guaranteed religious, political, and personal freedom. New states entering the Union modeled their constitutions after the U.S. Constitution that was created in Philadelphia and which was itself modeled on Pennsylvania's Great Law. In the wars that shaped our nation — the Revolutionary War and the Civil War — Pennsylvania was a key battleground.

In the decades following the Civil War, Pennsylvania was a leading source of our nation's strength. Coal from Pennsylvania's mines warmed and lit America's growing cities. Steel from Pennsylvania's mills built railroads, skyscrapers, and modern machines. The newcomers who arrived to work in Pennsylvania's industries helped make the United States the diverse nation it is today.

The nation stands tall because it is built on the ideals of the Keystone State. Pennsylvania's waterways and mountains were the blood and bones of a powerful nation, and its citizens — from Penn and "Poor Richard" to Cassatt, Cosby, and "Broadway Joe" Namath — fill fascinating pages in America's ongoing story.

▶ Map of Pennsylvania showing interstate highway system, as well as major cities and waterways.

▶ A statue of Commodore John Barry, father of the U.S. Navy, stands outside Independence Hall in Philadelphia.

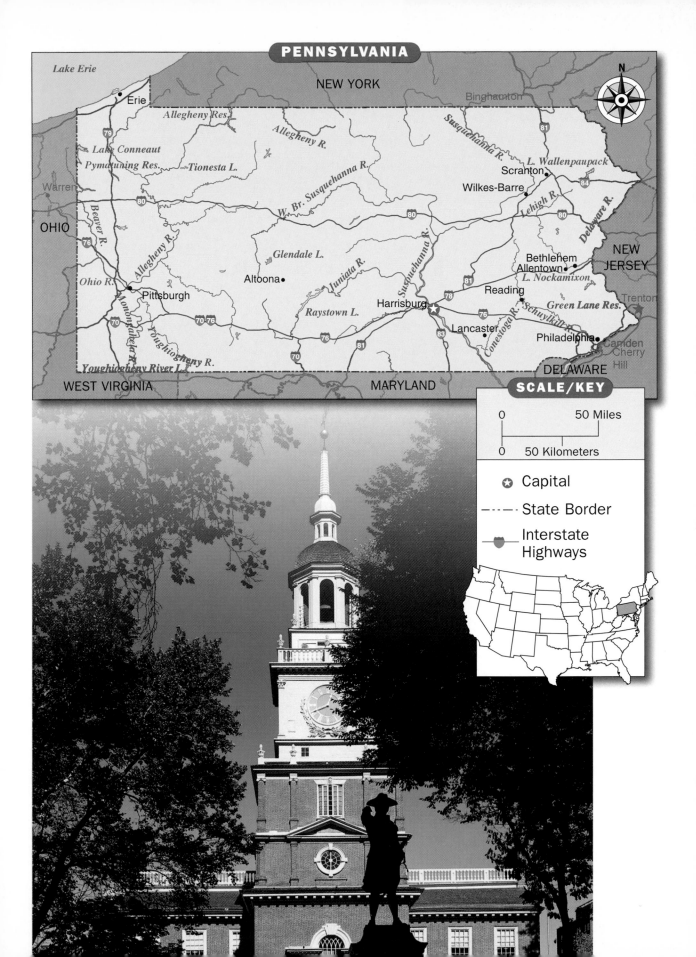

PENNSYLVANIA

Lake Erie

NEW YORK

Erie

Binghamton

Allegheny Res.

N

Allegheny R.

Susquehanna R.

L. Wallenpaupack

Lake Conneaut
Pymatuning Res.

Tionesta L.

Scranton

Wilkes-Barre

W. Br. Susquehanna R.

Lehigh R.

Delaware R.

Warren

OHIO

Beaver R.

Allegheny R.

Glendale L.

Altoona

Juniata R.

Susquehanna R.

Bethlehem
Allentown

L. Nockamixon

NEW
JERSEY

Ohio R.

Pittsburgh

Reading

Green Lane Res.

Trenton

Monongahela R.

Youghiogheny R.

Raystown L.

Harrisburg

Schuylkill R.

Conestoga R.

Lancaster

Philadelphia

Camden
Cherry
Hill

Youghiogheny River L.

WEST VIRGINIA

MARYLAND

DELAWARE

SCALE/KEY

| 0 | 50 Miles |

| 0 | 50 Kilometers |

⭐ Capital

----- State Border

 Interstate Highways

Fast Facts

PENNSYLVANIA (PA), The Keystone State

Entered Union
December 12, 1787 (2nd state)

Capital   Population
Harrisburg 48,950

Toatal Population
12,281,054 (6th most populous state)

Largest Cities   Population
Philadelphia 1,517,550
Pittsburgh 334,563
Allentown 106,632
Erie 103,717

Land Area
44,817 square miles (116,076 square kilometers) (32nd largest state)

State Motto
Virtue, Liberty, and Independence

State Song
"Pennsylvania" *by Eddie Khoury and Ronnie Bonner*

State Animal
Whitetail Deer

State Bird

Ruffed Grouse — *Perhaps it's possible to be too popular — when you're popular as a game bird! "Game" is a name given to animals that are hunted for food.*

State Fish
Brook Trout

State Insect
Firefly — *Why do fireflies glow? It's mainly to attract mates, but their light also warns predators about their bitter taste. There's no accounting for taste, though. Some frogs eat so many fireflies that they start glowing, too!*

State Tree

Hemlock

State Flower
Mountain Laurel — *Pennsylvania's choice for state flower was delayed when residents of western Pennsylvania supported the wild honeysuckle instead. Eastern Pennsylvanians rallied behind the mountain laurel and finally won out in 1933.*

State Dog
Great Dane — *This largest of state dogs was known to be the "best friend" of William Penn, the state founder. There's one in a famous painting that hangs in the governor's reception room.*

State Fossil
Phacops rana — *Students picked this variety of trilobite as the state fossil partly because its 1-inch (2.5-centimeter) long fossils are common in Pennsylvania. Also, its large head reminded them of Darth Vader from Star Wars.*

PLACES TO VISIT

The Liberty Bell
Independence National Historical Park, Philadelphia
Every year millions of visitors file past the familiar cracked bell, one of our nation's most

treasured relics. Rung on July 8, 1776, to celebrate the Declaration of Independence, the bell has become a symbol of national liberty.

Daniel Boone Homestead, *Birdsboro*
Daniel Boone was born here in 1734 and lived his first sixteen years in Berks County. The mid-eighteenth-century structure that survives today is built over the spring and cellar where the first Boone log cabin stood.

For other places and events, see p. 44

BIGGEST, BEST, AND MOST

- Many important documents of U.S. history were written in Pennsylvania. The Declaration of Independence and the U.S. Constitution were both written in Philadelphia.

STATE FIRSTS

- Nation's first museum of art — the Philadelphia Academy of Arts
- First natural history museum
- First hospital — the Pennsylvania Hospital
- First scientific society — the Franklin Institute, endowed by Benjamin Franklin
- First circulating library
- First medical college, founded in 1765 by John Morgan
- First regular steamboat run
- First locomotive on rails

Chocolate Town

After making his fortune with caramel, Milton S. Hershey turned his attention to chocolate. In 1905 he opened what is now the world's largest chocolate factory, even building a town around it that became known as Hershey, Pennsylvania. Hershey made chocolate milkier and sweeter to appeal to U.S. tastes and in the process made an even greater fortune. Most of that fortune went to the M. S. Hershey Foundation, which continues to support many charitable causes.

Hedgehog Day?

Punxsutawney, Pennsylvania, celebrates a custom on the second day of February that goes back to the early days of Christianity in Europe. If the sun shone on Candlemas Day, then a hedgehog would see its shadow — forecasting six more weeks of winter weather. Hedgehogs don't live in Pennsylvania, so German immigrants chose the groundhog instead. In 1887 Phil, the Punxsutawney Groundhog, was proclaimed the official weather-predicting groundhog. Phil's fame spread, and more people began to make the journey to Punxsutawney every year. With the release of the 1993 movie *Groundhog Day,* starring Bill Murray, the crowds began to number in the tens of thousands.

Birthplace of a Nation

> Pennsylvania, lying in the northern part of America, is a country of no small compass. It lies in a healthy climate; it is not merely inhabitable, but very much inhabited, not only by the ancient dwellers in the land, but also by thousands who have emigrated thither from Europe and still arrive every year.
>
> — *Michael Schlatter, Description of Pennsylvania*
> *Written at Amsterdam, 1751*

Pennsylvania's history began long before Europeans envisioned a country called the United States. Native Americans lived in the area we know as Pennsylvania as long as ten thousand years before the arrival of Europeans.

By the 1600s four major Native American tribes had settled primarily in eastern Pennsylvania — the Lenni Lenape (called the Delaware by Europeans), the Susquehannock, the Shawnee, and several tribes of the large and powerful Iroquois Confederacy.

The Lenni Lenape lived in the Delaware River Valley. The first European settlers from Sweden traveled upriver from the Delaware Bay in the mid-1600s. By the end of the 1600s the Delaware had moved west, first across the Allegheny Mountains and then on to eastern Ohio. During the French and Indian War (1754–1763), the Delaware fought on the side of the French. In the Revolutionary War they fought for the British. Today descendants of the Delaware live on reservations in Oklahoma as well as in Ontario, Canada.

The Susquehannock established villages along the Susquehanna River in southeastern Pennsylvania. Few Susquehannock survived the great Iroquois massacre of 1675. Most survivors later died from illnesses carried by European settlers.

The Shawnee people also lived along the Susquehanna River, near present-day Easton, Pennsylvania. Like the

Native Americans of Pennsylvania
Erie
Lenni Lenape (Delaware)
Mahican
Susquehannock
Shawnee
Iroquois Confederacy

Algonquian-speaking
Lenni Lenape
Mahican
Shawnee
Iroquoian-speaking
Erie
Iroquois Confederacy
Susquehannock

Delaware, they fought alongside the French in the French and Indian War, and with the British in the Revolutionary War. Most Shawnee descendants were relocated to Indiana or Oklahoma reservations.

Various groups of the powerful Iroquois Confederacy also lived in Pennsylvania. The Confederacy, formed in 1570, brought together Iroquois tribes such as the Mohawk, Cayuga, and Oneida. The Iroquois were widely feared as fierce and well-trained warriors. Throughout the 1600s the Iroquois tribes fought with Algonquian-speaking tribes, as well as among themselves.

Smaller Native American groups such as the Mahican also lived in Pennsylvania. Today about eleven thousand Native Americans live in Pennsylvania.

▲ The Declaration of Independence was signed in Philadelphia in 1776. John Trumbull painted this picture of the event between 1788 and 1795.

Early European Settlements

The first European to explore the area now known as Pennsylvania was Captain John Smith of Virginia, in 1608. The first Europeans to settle the region, however, were the Swedish. Johan Printz established the colony of New Sweden on Tinicum Island in 1643. The Dutch, however, claimed that Henry Hudson's voyage into Delaware Bay in 1609 had given them first rights of settlement. The Dutch gained control in 1655. Dutch dominance of the region ended when the English seized it in 1664.

The Quaker Colony

King Charles II and the crown owed a huge financial debt to Admiral Sir William Penn. Penn's son, also named William, requested land in the colonies as repayment. Penn was a member of the Society of Friends, known as the Quakers. He wanted to establish a colony for his fellow Quakers, who were being persecuted in England for their refusal to fight in wars and their rejection of traditional religion. The King issued a charter giving William Penn the territory between the provinces of Maryland and New York. The land was named in honor of Penn's father — *Pennsylvania* means "Penn's Woods" — and the Charter of Pennsylvania was signed on March 4, 1681.

What's in a Name

Delaware, the name by which the Lenni Lenape came to be known, is not Native American in origin. In fact, the term, which names a tribe, a bay, a river, and a state, is credited to English explorer Captain Samuel Argall.

While sailing along the Atlantic coast north of Jamestown in 1610, Argall's ship entered a large bay that he named after Sir Thomas West, Third Lord de la Warr, the English noble who served as the first governor of Virginia.

▼ A northbound Conrail train carries freight across the Susquehanna River.

Penn envisioned a colony based on religious freedom, tolerance, and independence. The *First Frame of Government* was his proposed Pennsylvania Constitution. Penn arrived in America in 1682 and began laying out a new city on the Delaware River. He called it Philadelphia, which means the "City of Brotherly Love."

Penn called a General Assembly and pushed for the adoption of the Great Law, a document that guaranteed freedom of conscience. People were allowed to live as they wished and to practice the religion of their choice. Citizens also had rights to life, liberty, and ownership of land. This law became the basis for the Declaration of Independence and the U.S. Constitution.

Colonial Expansion and Turmoil

As the Pennsylvania colony grew larger, it faced increased problems with Native Americans who had begun to resent and resist growing European expansion. The English settled primarily in the southeast, making the port of Philadelphia the most important city in colonial America by the mid-1700s. German immigrants seeking religious freedom arrived in large numbers and turned south central Pennsylvania into prosperous farming country. Adventurous Scots-Irish settlers headed for the frontiers of western Pennsylvania. Many new immigrant groups engaged in slavery. About four thousand Africans had been brought to Pennsylvania as slaves by 1730.

As a colony of Great Britain, Pennsylvania played a pivotal role in the French and Indian War (1754–1763). The French joined forces with Native Americans against the British for control of the region. Many battles took place in Pennsylvania, including George Washington's first military victory leading pro-British colonial troops. British forces eventually won out, securing the region for England.

Shortly after the French and Indian War, a united group of Native Americans attacked a

Benjamin Franklin
1706–1790

Benjamin Franklin, born in poverty in Boston in 1706, became one of colonial Pennsylvania's most famous citizens, successful enough to retire by age forty. He arrived in Philadelphia at age twenty-three and within ten years had founded the first library, fire department, and insurance company in America. A printer, publisher, author, scientist, and statesman, Franklin became the model of the resourceful, do-it-yourself American, possibly the most famous American in the world by the time of the Revolution. He invented the Franklin stove, bifocal glasses, and the lightning rod. Franklin also wrote the first autobiography published in the United States. Franklin signed the Declaration of Independence and during the Revolution was largely responsible for persuading the French to give military and financial aid to the colonists' cause. He died in Philadelphia, the new nation's capital, on April 17, 1790.

British settlement in the brief conflict known as Pontiac's War. They were defeated at the Battle of Bushy Run in August 1763, thus ending all conflict between Native Americans and settlers in Pennsylvania. A proclamation in that same year promised Native Americans that there would be limits on westward expansion of Europeans. Settlement continued west in Pennsylvania, however, because of expanding trade routes that reached the Ohio River.

Throughout the 1770s Philadelphia was the home of the movement for U.S. independence. The First Continental Congress met in Independence Hall on September 5, 1774, to agree on a response to the Intolerable Acts passed by Great Britain. These laws tightened control over the colonies with a series of taxes and regulations. The members of the first Congress included such famous figures as George Washington, John Adams, John Jay, and Patrick Henry. The Congress issued a Declaration of Personal Rights that outlined the principles of life, liberty, property, assembly, and trial by jury. They also denounced "taxation without representation" and the forced housing of British soldiers in private homes.

The Mason-Dixon Line

In 1763 British surveyors Jeremiah Dixon and Charles Mason were commissioned to establish the boundary between Pennsylvania and Maryland. They placed milestones with a "P" on one side and an "M" on the other. The Mason–Dixon Line was considered the boundary between "free" and "slave" states. In truth, the line simply defines the border between two states.

▼ William Penn's treaties with Native Americans helped his state to flourish in the colonial era.

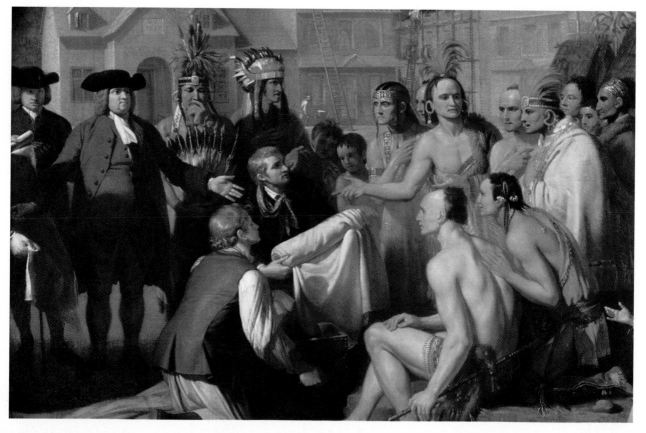

Declaring Independence

The Second Continental Congress met in Philadelphia in May 1775 to take up the cause of independence from England. That Congress appointed George Washington as commander in chief of the American army in June of 1775. It also acted as the new government of the thirteen colony-states, issuing and borrowing money, establishing a postal service, and creating a navy. New members of the Second Congress included Benjamin Franklin and Thomas Jefferson.

With a committee's advice, Jefferson wrote the Declaration of Independence over several weeks in late June 1776. Approved on July 4 and signed later by the delegates of the Second Continental Congress, it is one of history's most famous documents.

In 1787 Philadelphia was once again the site of the creation of a famous document, the U.S. Constitution. Pennsylvania was the second state to ratify the document and join the United States of America. Philadelphia became the capital of the United States from 1790 until 1800, when Washington, D.C., became the capital.

The Abolitionists and the Civil War

In 1781 the Pennsylvania Emancipation Act promised the gradual abolition of slavery in the state — the first state document to do so in the United States. Pennsylvanians were divided over the issue. A critical problem in the state was the return of runaway slaves to their masters. Pennsylvania's border with Maryland also marked the dividing line between slave and free states. Thus, many slaves escaped northward into Pennsylvania throughout the first half of the 1800s. African Americans Robert Porter and William Still, both Pennsylvanians, were the driving forces behind the establishment of the Underground Railroad that helped slaves escape.

In 1856 James Buchanan was elected the fifteenth U.S. president and so far the only president from Pennsylvania. Buchanan had a policy of noninterference with slavery, heightening tension between the opposing sides. Buchanan served only one term before giving way to Abraham Lincoln.

Pennsylvania played a critical role in U.S. history during the Civil War (1861–1865). In July 1863 Confederate troops were turned back at the Battle of Gettysburg, the costliest battle in U.S. military history, with more than fifty

Andrew Carnegie

▲ Scottish immigrant, Andrew Carnegie was a major figure in Pennsylvania's steel industry after the Civil War. As a young man Carnegie worked for the Pennsylvania Railroad, investing his money in the railroad as it expanded and thus building a small fortune. In the early 1870s Carnegie began to build steel mills. As the mills grew larger, Carnegie also took ownership of the mines that produced iron ore for steel as well as the rail lines that carried the ore to his mills. Carnegie became one of the wealthiest men in the world, eventually selling the Carnegie Steel Corporation to the U.S. Steel Corporation for $250 million in 1901 — an enormous sum. Carnegie vowed to help society with his fortune. He spent the rest of his life managing his charitable organization, The Carnegie Foundation, which established a number of public libraries across the United States.

thousand casualties. Although the war continued for nearly two more years, Gettysburg was widely considered the turning point. President Lincoln delivered his immortal Gettysburg Address at a dedication of the battlefield cemetery. Nearly 350,000 Pennsylvanians served in the Union forces, including 8,600 African-American volunteers.

▲ Valley Forge was the winter camp for Revolutionary War soldiers commanded by George Washington.

Coal, Oil, Iron, and Steel

The discovery of enormous deposits of two important natural resources, coal and oil, solidified Pennsylvania's economic power. In 1820 mining companies began digging deposits of hard and soft coal from veins deep in the Appalachian Mountains. In 1859 Edwin Drake drilled the first successful oil well at Titusville. Pennsylvania soon became the nation's leading oil producer and refiner.

The future of the state's industry, however, lay in iron and steel. By 1860 Pennsylvania factories produced about half of the nation's iron.

During the second half of the nineteenth century, immigrants from eastern and southern Europe arrived in huge numbers to work in the mines and mills of the state. They settled in cities such as Pittsburgh, Bethlehem, Harrisburg, Lewistown, and Carlisle.

Many of Pennsylvania's steel companies combined into the giant U.S. Steel Corporation. Through its sheer size, it dominated the industry, producing steel and mining coal, coke, limestone, and iron ore. In the 1900s western Pennsylvania also became a major aluminum producer.

Pennsylvania's huge iron and steel industries, and its huge number of immigrant laborers, led to the state's development as a center of the labor union movement. Labor unrest led to riots in Pittsburgh during the Great Railroad Strike of 1877. Other important strikes occurred in the steel industry in 1892 and 1919. From such unrest arose two of the nation's most powerful unions, the United Mine Workers and the United Steelworkers of America.

The Twentieth Century

Pennsylvania's economy in the 1900s was troubled. While steel, weapons, and machinery production was crucial during the two world wars, the state experienced economic decline in the postwar era and in the final decades of the twentieth century.

Pennsylvania led the way in nuclear power development. The town of Shippingport was the site of the world's first nuclear power plant, opened in 1957. Unfortunately, the first major nuclear accident in the United States also occurred in Pennsylvania, at Three Mile Island in 1979.

Pennsylvania has faced the realities of economic decline with a combination of ingenuity and resolve. Bolstered in part by revivals in the service and high-technology industries, the Keystone State is ready to take on the future.

Birthplace of a Nation: Revolutionary Pennsylvania

By the time of the American Revolution, Pennsylvania, especially its capital, Philadelphia, had become the center of military, economic, and cultural activity in the colonies. In fact, by 1770 Philadelphia was the second-largest English-speaking city in the world after London. Due to its location between the northern and southern colonies, Philadelphia became the gathering point for the leaders who created the new nation. The city was the meeting site of the First (1774) and Second (1775–81) Continental Congresses. The Declaration of Independence was written and signed there in 1776. The Constitution was created in the city in 1787. In 1790 Philadelphia became the capital of the United States and served as the nation's capital until 1800.

▶ Radioactive gases were vented after a valve malfunctioned at the Three Mile Island nuclear power plant in 1979.

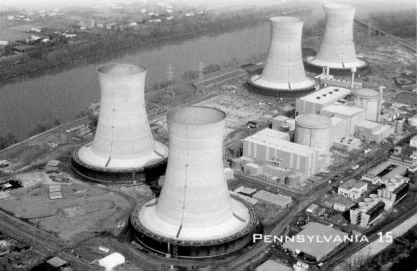

Society of Friends

> The journeymen were inquisitive where I had been, what sort of a country it was, and how I lik'd it. I prais'd it [Philadelphia] much, the happy life I led in it, expressing strongly my intention of returning to it . . .
>
> — *Benjamin Franklin, 1771*

Benjamin Franklin's positive view of Philadelphia is an attitude long shared by citizens across the Keystone State. Even at the dawn of U.S. history, the city and the entire state were popular destinations for new arrivals from Europe.

Who Lives in Pennsylvania?

Settlements within the state tended to arise near the state's waterways. The two largest cities — Philadelphia and Pittsburgh — lie at opposite ends of the state, but both are located on major waterways. More than 25 percent of all Pennsylvanians live in or around these two cities.

Pennsylvania's largest population groups include people of German, Irish, Italian, and English descent. About 10 percent of the Pennsylvanians are African American. Other

Age Distribution in Pennsylvania

0–4	727,804
5–19	2,542,780
20–24	746,086
25–44	,508,562
45–64	2,836,657
65 and over	1,919,165

Across One Hundred Years

Pennsylvania's three largest foreign-born groups for 1890 and 1990

1890			1990		
Ireland	Germany	England	United Kingdom	Germany	Italy
243,836	230,516	125,089	25,214	24,359	18,808

Total state population: 5,258,014
Total foreign-born: 845,720 (16%)

Total state population: 11,881,643
Total foreign-born: 369,316 (3%)

Patterns of Immigration

The total number of people who immigrated to Pennsylvania in 1998 was 11,942. Of that number, the largest immigrant groups were from India (9%), China (8%) and Mexico (5%).

large groups include people of Polish, Slovak, and Dutch descent.

Although the state's population is diverse, Pennsylvania today is the state with the most native-born residents. In other words, families that settle in Pennsylvania stay there. The state's median age is thirty-eight, placing it among the five "oldest" states in the country. In fact, almost 75 percent of the population is over twenty-one, and nearly 20 percent is over sixty-two.

▲ In early May runners compete in the Pittsburgh Marathon.

Freedom and Opportunity

Religious freedom and economic opportunity have drawn immigrants to Pennsylvania from a wide range of cultures throughout the world. The first Jewish synagogue in Philadelphia was established in 1740. By that time there were about four thousand African-American slaves in the state. Pennsylvania was the first state to abolish slavery, and by 1860 more than fifty thousand African Americans lived in Philadelphia, making it a population and cultural center of African-American life.

> **DID YOU KNOW?**
>
> **A**lthough more than 70 percent of Pennsylvanians live in urban or suburban areas, the state still has the largest rural population of any state.

Heritage and Background, Pennsylvania · Year 2000

▶ Here's a look at the racial backgrounds of Pennsylvanians today. Pennsylvania ranks twenty-first among all U.S. states with regard to African Americans as a percentage of the population.

White
10,484,203
85.4%

Native Hawaiian and Other Pacific Islander
3,417
0.0%

Total population
12,281,054

Note: 3.2% (394,088) of the population identify themselves as **Hispanic** or **Latino,** a cultural designation that crosses racial lines. Hispanics and Latinos are counted in this category and the racial category of their choice.

American Indian and Alaska Native
18,348
0.1%

Two or more races
142,224
1.2%

Some other race
188,437
1.5%

Asian
219,813
1.8%

Black or African American
1,224,612
10.0%

Pennsylvania originated as a tolerant location of "brotherly love," and the state drew large numbers of religious sects persecuted for their beliefs in their homeland. The Quakers were the first to seek that freedom, but the best known of these groups may be the "Pennsylvania Dutch," who settled in the rich farmlands of south–central Pennsylvania in the 1690s and 1700s. These people are actually of German descent. The majority belong to the so-called Plain Sects, Protestant groups that follow simple ways of dress and living. The most recognizable of these are the Amish, who do not use electricity, telephones, or automobiles. Amish fields are still cultivated by horse-drawn plows, and the Amish dress in plain, black-and-white clothing and hold worship services in each other's homes.

Education

Education has been highly regarded throughout Pennsylvania's history. The Great Law stated that children

Educational Level of Pennsylvania Workers	
Less than 9th grade	741,167
9th to 12th grade, no diploma	1,253,111
High school graduate, including equivalency	3,035,080
Some college, no degree	1,017,897
Associate degree	412,931
Bachelor's degree	890,660
Graduate or professional degree	522,086

▼ The city of Philadelphia sparkles on the banks of the Delaware River.

should know how to read and write by the age of twelve, an unusual attitude at a time when more than half of all colonists, including most women, were illiterate, even by the year 1800. The Friends' Public School, founded in Philadelphia by Quakers in 1689, still exists as the William Penn Charter School.

▲ An Amish family travels in a horse-drawn vehicle.

The State Constitution of 1790 required the legislature to establish schools for the children of poor parents. In 1834 the Free School Act was passed. It established school districts throughout the state, making Pennsylvania the second state in the nation to offer public school to its residents. Today state law requires children from ages eight through sixteen to attend school.

Pennsylvania has also long been famous for its many institutions of higher learning. There are more than two hundred two- and four-year colleges and universities throughout the state. The University of Pennsylvania in Philadelphia, established in 1753 as the Philadelphia Academy by (who else?) Benjamin Franklin, was the country's first nondenominational university.

Religion

Although Pennsylvania was founded by Quakers, they did not long remain a majority in the state. Today Quakers represent 0.1 percent of the population. The state is also famous for its "Pennsylvania Dutch" population, who are members of several churches known collectively as Plain Sects. More than seventy-five thousand people in Lancaster County belong to Plain Sects, such as the Amish, Mennonite, and Brethren churches. About one-third of Pennsylvanians are Catholic, and nearly 10 percent Baptist. Almost 9 percent of Pennsylvanians belong to Methodist churches and more than 5 percent are Presbyterians. Among Pennsylvanians who are not Christian, 2.3 percent are Jewish and 0.3 percent Muslim. Agnostics, who believe that there is no way to prove or disprove the existence of God, make up 0.7 percent of the population.

A Land of Water and Stone

> Still the pine-woods scent the noon;
> Still the catbird sings his tune;
> Still the autumn sets the maple forest blazing . . .
> Still the fire-flies in the corn make night amazing
>
> — *from "Philadelphia," by Rudyard Kipling*

When looking at a landscape map of Pennsylvania two words come to mind, *rivers* and *mountains*. Even though Pennsylvania is called a Middle Atlantic State, it is the only one of the five — Delaware, New Jersey, New York, Pennsylvania, and Maryland — that does not touch the Atlantic Ocean.

Rivers and Ports

Ocean border or not, water has been key to the state's development. Pennsylvania has more than 45,000 miles (72,000 kilometers) of rivers that create three major ports in the state. Philadelphia, situated at the point where the Schuykill flows into the much larger Delaware River, is the world's largest freshwater port. In the northwest the port city of Erie, on Lake Erie, connects the state to the Great Lakes, allowing travel to the Midwest or to the Atlantic along the St. Lawrence Seaway. The western city Pittsburgh, located at the point where the Allegheny and Monongahela Rivers join to form the mighty Ohio River, is one of the busiest inland ports in the United States.

▼ *From left to right:* the Delaware river; Berks County farm land; Bowman's Hill; spring in Bucks County; a Pennsylvania fox kit; Pocono mountain scenery.

Mountains

The rivers flow between spines of mountain ridges that run northeast to southwest across Pennsylvania. Originally part of a vast inland sea, these rounded mountains were formed by massive movements of Earth's crust millions of years ago and shaped again by retreating glaciers thousands of years ago. Beneath these rocky ridges prehistoric swamplands have been compressed into the world's greatest source of anthracite coal.

Climate

Pennsylvania's climate, like most climates in the Middle Atlantic, covers a wide range without reaching extremes of temperature or precipitation. Summers can run from warm to extremely humid. Winter snows often cover the landscape in the north of the state as well as at higher elevations. Temperatures rarely dip below 10°F (-12°C).

Land Areas

Pennsylvania is shaped roughly like a rectangle. Rivers and mountains fill most of that shape, with the only flat areas occurring on the upper left and lower right areas of the shape. The state lies in a large area of the eastern United States known as the Appalachian Highlands, which has some the most densely forested areas of the country. In fact, forests cover about 60 percent of the state.

Geographers divide Pennsylvania into seven regions: (1) Erie Lowland, (2) Allegheny Plateau, (3) Appalachian Ridge and Valley Region, (4) Blue Ridge, (5) Piedmont, (6) New England Upland, and (7) Atlantic Coastal Plain. The Erie Lowland is a narrow strip in the northwestern corner of Pennsylvania on Lake Erie's shores, connecting the state to New York and Ohio. Vegetables and fruits grow well in the sandy soil of this region.

Average January temperature
Philadelphia: 34.5°F (1.4°C)
Pittsburgh: 36.2°F (2.3°C)

Average July temperature
Philadelphia: 77.9°F (25.5°C)
Pittsburgh: 72°F (22.2°C)

Average yearly rainfall
Philadelphia: 41 inches (104.3 cm)
Pittsburgh: 36.8 inches (93.4 cm)

Average yearly snowfall
Philadelphia: 20.4 inches (51.8 cm)
Pittsburgh: 43.3 inches (109.9 cm)

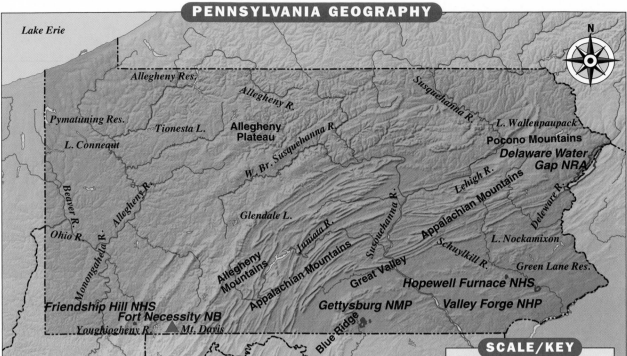

Lake Erie
Allegheny Res.
Pymatuning Res.
Tionesta L.
Allegheny Plateau
Allegheny R.
W. Br. Susquehanna R.
Susquehanna R.
Susquehanna R.
L. Wallenpaupack
Pocono Mountains
Delaware Water Gap NRA
L. Conneaut
Beaver R.
Allegheny R.
Ohio R.
Monongahela R.
Glendale L.
Juniata R.
Allegheny Mountains
Appalachian Mountains
Susquehanna R.
Great Valley
Lehigh R.
Appalachian Mountains
Schuylkill R.
Delaware R.
L. Nockamixon
Green Lane Res.
Hopewell Furnace NHS
Valley Forge NHP
Friendship Hill NHS
Fort Necessity NB
Youghiogheny R.
Mt. Davis
Gettysburg NMP
Blue Ridge

SCALE/KEY

0		50 Miles
0	50 Kilometers	

NB National Battlefield

NHS National Historic Site

NMP National Memorial Park

NRA National Resource Area

▲ Highest Point

Mountains

The Allegheny Plateau covers the northern and western region of the state. This land area is made up of narrow valleys and plateaulike ridges that are the source of many of the state's rivers. These plateaus reach elevations of 2,000 feet (610 meters). The Allegheny Mountains, on the eastern edge of the plateau, run from north-central Pennsylvania southwest to West Virginia and Virginia. Mount Davis, the state's highest point, rises to 3,213 feet (979 m) at the southern border.

The Appalachian Ridge and Valley Region in Pennsylvania is a wide strip of land south and east of the Allegheny Plateau. An area called the Great Valley extends across the southeastern ridge and valley region. The Great Valley is divided into the smaller Cumberland, Lebanon, and Lehigh valleys, all regions with fertile farmland. North and west of these valleys are parallel ridges of sedimentary rock formed from deposits of ancient rivers and lakes. The Pocono Mountains, long a popular tourist destination, are set in the northeastern part of this region.

Erosion has worn down the softer rock layers, forming the Delaware Water Gap along the Pennsylvania–New Jersey boundary. This region of the state contains the

High Point

Mt. Davis
3,213 feet (979 m)

Pocono Mounatins
1,800 feet (550 m)

anthracite coal fields and slate formations that were a major part of the state's mining industry.

The Blue Ridge, part of the much larger Blue Ridge Mountains, forms a narrow, finger-shaped region at the state's south-central border. Scenic South Mountain, picturesque Buchanan Valley, and part of Gettysburg National Military Park are located in this region.

The Piedmont region in Pennsylvania covers the southeastern part of the state. This region of rolling plains and low hills has some of the richest farmland in the United States. The New England Uplands are a narrow rectangle in eastern Pennsylvania.

The Atlantic Coastal Plain is a narrow strip of land in the southeastern corner of the state. The region is at sea level along the Delaware River, where Philadelphia is located.

Lakes and Rivers

There are three major river systems in Pennsylvania. Along the eastern border of the state is the Delaware River. Its two chief branches are the Schuykill and the Lehigh. In the east-central part of the state, two branches of the Susquehanna River meet to flow southward through Maryland into Chesapeake Bay. At Pittsburgh the Allegheny and the Monongahela meet to form the Ohio River.

Largest Lakes

Pymatuning Reservoir
26 square miles
(67 square kilometers)

Raystown Lake
13 square miles
(34 square kilometers)

Lake Conneaut
1.5 square miles
(3.9 square kilometers)

Major Rivers

Ohio River
981 miles (1,579 km) long

Susquehanna
447 miles (719 km) long

Delaware
390 miles (627 km) long

Allegheny River
325 miles (523 km) long

Monongahela
130 miles (210 km) long

Conestoga River
114 miles (184 km) long

◀ Cannons serve as a reminder of the pivotal Civil War battle fought at Gettysburg.

A Changing Economy

The forces of the Nineteenth Century are Capital and Labor, united they transform the desert into a garden, in collision they convert the garden into a waste. On the 6th of July, 1892, at Homestead, Penn., the Forces met. The sound of the shock echoed through the labor markets of the world.

— *From the July 16, 1892, issue of* Illustrated American

Pennsylvania has been a prosperous industrial state for most of its history due to natural resources and large population. Many navigable rivers in the state and miles of rail lines and roads gave the Keystone State an advantage in delivering goods to markets. In the 1700s and 1800s, Pennsylvania was second only to New York in economic wealth. Although industry and labor clashed over working conditions in the early 1900s, the state remained an economic power for several decades after World War II.

Manufacturing to Service

Until about 1970 Pennsylvania's economy was driven by the manufacture of steel and machinery, which are still produced there. The top manufactured products in the state today are electrical equipment and chemicals.

The combination of changing markets, environmental concerns, and technological development, however, has transformed Pennsylvania into a service-based economy. More than one-third of Pennsylvania's workforce of almost six million people work in service-related jobs, which include banking, health care, and retail sales. Given the state's natural beauty and long history, many service industries benefit from tourism.

Top Employers
(in order of number of workers employed)

Service	24.8%
Wholesale and retail trade	20.1%
Manufacturing	17.8%
Government	12.2%
Finance, insurance, and real estate	6.1%
Transportation and public utilities	5.6%
Construction	4.1%
Agriculture	1.6%

DID YOU KNOW?

Retail Tales — John Wanamaker opened the nation's first department store, Wanamaker's, in Philadelphia in the 1870s. Frank Woolworth opened his first five-and-dime stores in Lancaster, Pennsylvania, at the same time.

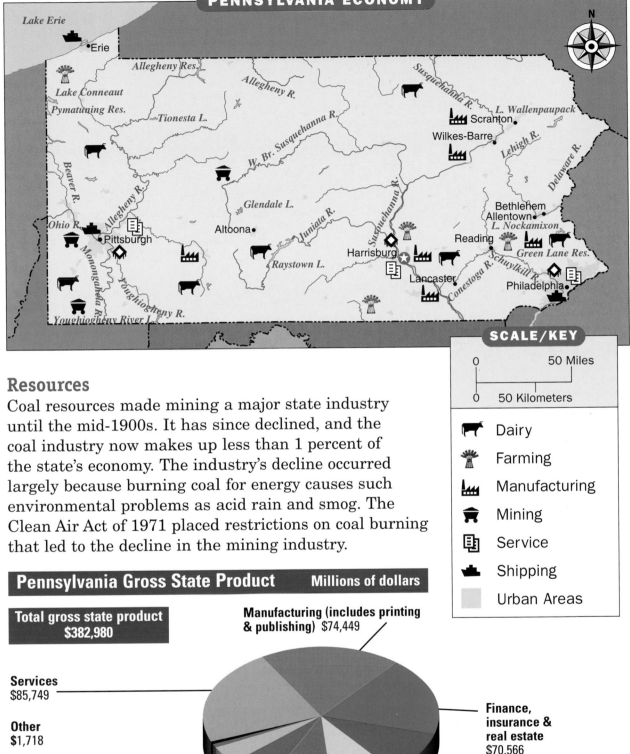

Resources

Coal resources made mining a major state industry until the mid-1900s. It has since declined, and the coal industry now makes up less than 1 percent of the state's economy. The industry's decline occurred largely because burning coal for energy causes such environmental problems as acid rain and smog. The Clean Air Act of 1971 placed restrictions on coal burning that led to the decline in the mining industry.

SCALE/KEY

0	50 Miles
0	50 Kilometers

🐂 Dairy
🌾 Farming
🏭 Manufacturing
⛏ Mining
🏢 Service
🚢 Shipping
　 Urban Areas

Pennsylvania Gross State Product — Millions of dollars

Total gross state product $382,980

Manufacturing (includes printing & publishing) $74,449

Services $85,749

Other $1,718

Mining $2,593

Agriculture, forestry, fishing, farms, agricultural services $1,636

Construction $16,079

Wholesale trade $23,826

Retail trade $34,359

Transportation & utilities $32,935

Government $39,070

Finance, insurance & real estate $70,566

Did You Know?

Despite general declines in the coal-mining industry, the coal mines of eastern Pennsylvania provide about 8 million tons of clean-burning anthracite (hard coal) every year. Pennsylvania is the only state that mines anthracite.

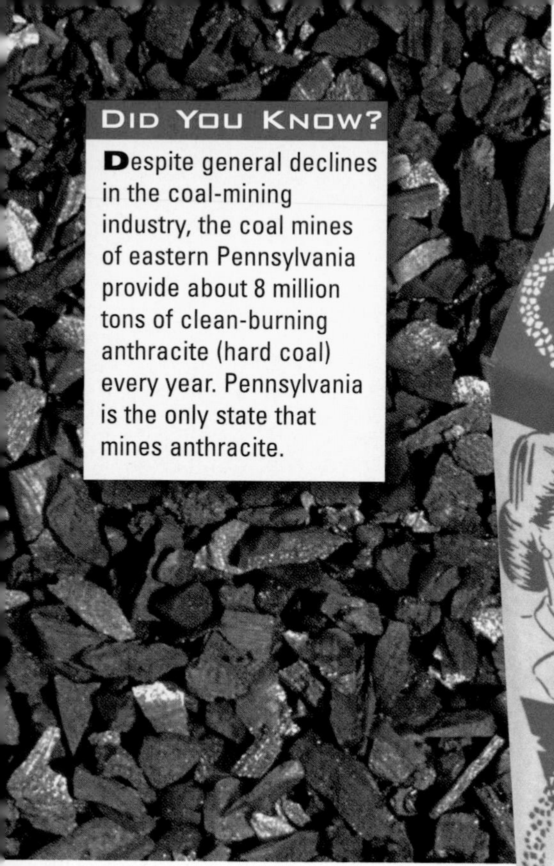

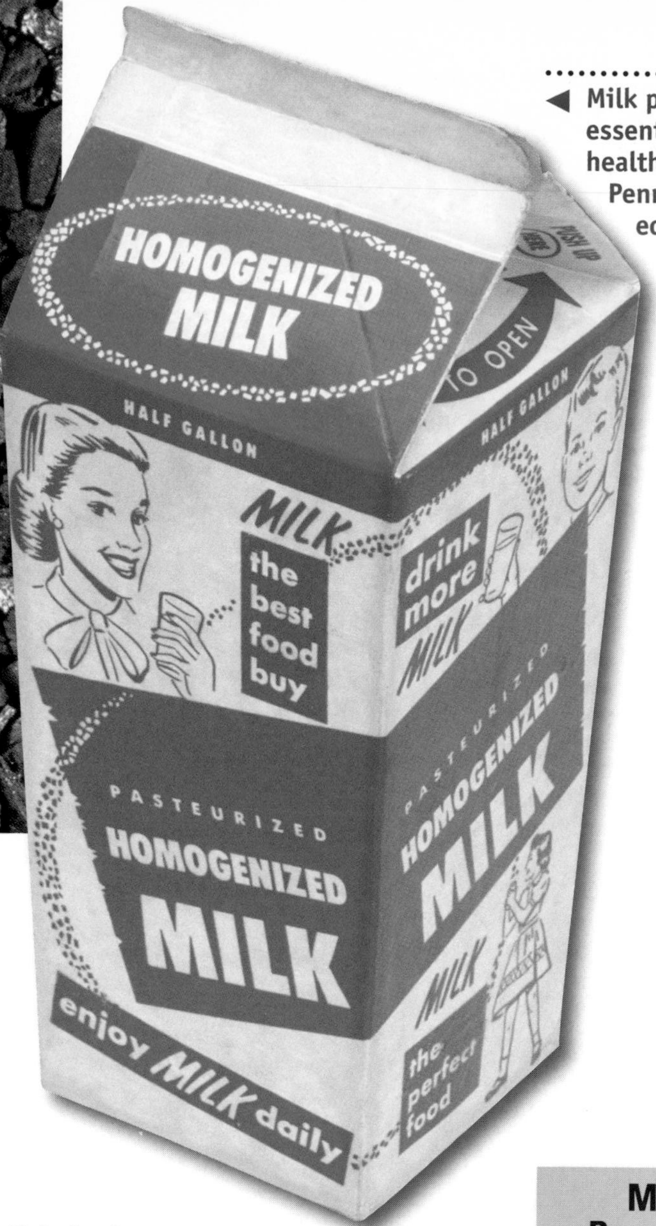

◀ Milk production is essential to the health of the Pennsylvania economy.

Among the state's other natural resources, limestone and natural gas are most important. Western Pennsylvania is the source of almost all of the state's natural gas.

Agriculture

Farmland covers about one-third of Pennsylvania's land area. The state has about fifty thousand farms and the largest rural population in the United States. Livestock such as cattle and livestock products such as milk account for almost 70 percent of Pennsylvania's farm income. Milk is the state's leading agricultural product. Dairy farming is primarily centered in eastern Pennsylvania.

Cattle, second in value of livestock products, are raised mainly along the Susquehanna River in the southeastern part of the state. That region of the state also has many poultry farms; Pennsylvania ranks among the leading egg-producing states.

Made in Pennsylvania

Leading farm products and crops
Milk and dairy
Livestock
Mushrooms
Apples
Peaches
Corn
Hay

Other products
Electrical equipment
Pharmaceuticals
Ships
Concrete

Crops bring in about 30 percent of the state's farm income. Pennsylvania is the national leader in mushroom production. Corn and hay, used mainly to feed beef cattle, are the leading field crops. Other important crops are oats, potatoes, soybeans, and wheat. Pennsylvania's main fruit crops are apples and peaches, which are grown in the southern areas of the state. Cherries, grapes, and strawberries are also valuable fruit crops.

Transportation

Pennsylvania's inland waterways are among the most important in the eastern United States. Pittsburgh is the hub of the state waterways. From there, goods can be shipped on the Ohio, Monongahela, and Allegheny Rivers. Oceangoing ships can sail north up the Delaware River as far as Philadelphia. Philadelphia ranks as one of the United States' leading port cities. Finally, Pennsylvania's shore along Lake Erie provides access to the Great Lakes.

Pennsylvania has been a leader in ground transportation since colonial times. At the outbreak of the Civil War, the Keystone State had more miles of railroad and surfaced road than any state, north or south. The Pennsylvania Railroad, chartered in 1846, was a major factor in the development of Pennsylvania's steel industry. The nation's first major surfaced road, called a "turnpike," connected Philadelphia and Lancaster in 1794. The first section of the modern Pennsylvania Turnpike was completed in 1940. It was later extended east to New Jersey, west to Ohio, and north from Philadelphia to Scranton.

Ask any guitar player to name the best acoustic guitars made anywhere, and chances are that "Martin" will be the answer. The Martin Guitar Company of Nazareth, Pennsylvania, has been making acoustic wooden guitars for 168 years. Today the company produces about fifty thousand guitars every year — about 150 to 200 a day. Each guitar requires more than three hundred separate steps, and one guitar takes about three months to build!

Founded in 1833 by German immigrant C. F. Martin, the company is now run by Chris Martin IV — the sixth generation Martin to head the business.

International Airports		
Airport	Location	Passengers per year (2000)
Philadelphia International	Philadelphia	24,918,276
Pittsburgh International	Pittsburgh	20,556,075
Harrisburg International	Harrisburg	1,200,000

Reform Pioneer

> Nor shall he or she at any time be compelled to frequent or maintaine any religious worshipp place or ministry contrary to his or her mind . . .
>
> — *The Great Law, Pennsylvania's first constitution, 1682*

There is probably no state with a longer tradition of "American" liberty than Pennsylvania. The concept of the right of citizens to "life, liberty, and the pursuit of happiness," stated in the Declaration of Independence echoes the beliefs stated almost one hundred years earlier in William Penn's document that established freedom — within certain boundaries of behavior — for citizens of Pennsylvania.

Pennsylvania was the second state to ratify the U.S. Constitution. In its own history the state has had five constitutions. The most recent document was adopted in 1968. Earlier constitutions had been adopted in 1776, 1790, 1838, and 1874.

Constitutional amendments, or changes in the document, can be adopted in two ways. In one case an amendment can be proposed by a member of the state legislature. The amendment must be approved by a majority of both houses of the legislature. It must then be approved in a similar manner by the next elected legislature. To achieve final ratification, an amendment must be approved by a majority of the people voting on it in the next general election.

Amendments also can be proposed by a constitutional convention. Before a constitutional convention can meet, however, a majority of both legislative houses and state voters must approve it.

Pennsylvania had a one-house, or *unicameral*, legislature from the General Assembly of 1682 until 1790. At that point the new state constitution replaced this system with a bicameral House and Senate.

Three Capitals

Pennsylvania is one of the few states to have had more than one capital city. In addition, it is the only state to have had a state capital and a national capital in the same city. The city, of course, was Philadelphia, the first capital of the state of Pennsylvania and the capital of the United States from 1790–1800. Pennsylvania's state capital was moved to Lancaster in 1799. In 1812, Harrisburg became the state capital, and it has remained the seat of state government since then.

Executive Branch

Pennsylvania's governor, the chief executive of the state, is elected to a four-year term. A person may not serve as governor more than two terms in a row. The governor appoints the secretary of the commonwealth, also known as the secretary of state, the adjutant general, and other administrative officials. Other executive branch offices elected by voters are the lieutenant governor, attorney general, state treasurer, and auditor general. These officials also serve four-year terms. They may serve an unlimited number of terms, but not more than two terms in a row.

Legislative Branch

The Legislative branch of state government is called the General Assembly. This body is comprised of a 50-member Senate and a 203-member House of Representatives. Voters in the state's 50 senatorial districts elect one senator. Voters in the 203 representative districts elect one representative. Senators serve four-year terms, and representatives serve two-year terms. Every other year, on the first Tuesday in January, legislative sessions begin. They last for two years and end either on November 30 or whenever business is completed, whichever comes first. Sessions are usually held on Monday, Tuesday, and Wednesday, but the governor may call special sessions.

Judicial Branch

Pennsylvania's highest court is the state Supreme Court. This court is comprised of seven justices who are elected to ten-year terms. The justices may be approved for an additional ten-year term in a general election. The justice with the longest continuous length of service becomes the chief justice.

Below the Supreme Court are the state Superior Court and the Commonwealth Court. These are known as intermediate appellate courts.

▼ The vaulted dome of the Pennsylvania capitol building, in Harrisburg, was modeled after St. Peter's Basilica in Rome.

The Supreme Court, Superior Court, and Commonwealth Court meet yearly in Harrisburg, Pittsburgh, and Philadelphia. The Superior Court is served by fifteen judges, and the Commonwealth Court by nine. These judges are also elected to ten-year terms and may be reelected.

The trial courts of Pennsylvania fall into sixty districts, each with a Court of Common Pleas.

Local Government

Pennsylvania is unusual in that it has four different systems of local government units: counties, townships, cities, and boroughs. Sixty-two of the state's sixty-seven counties are governed by a three-member board of commissioners elected to four-year terms. Some large cities in the state, such as Philadelphia, consolidate city and county government. The mayor and a seventeen-member council govern both the city and the surrounding county.

Elected Posts in the Executive Branch		
Office	**Length of Term**	**Term Limits**
Governor	4 years	2 consecutive terms in 12 years
Lieutenant Governor	4 years	2 consecutive terms in 12 years
Attorney General	4 years	2 consecutive terms in 12 years
Secretary of Commonwealth	4 years	2 consecutive terms in 12 years
State Treasurer	4 years	2 consecutive terms in 12 years

After terrorist attacks struck the United States in 2001, President George W. Bush appointed Pennsylvania governor Tom Ridge to the newly created post of Director of Homeland Security. Ridge was sworn in on October 8, 2001. The terrorist attacks affected Ridge's home state — one of the four airliners hijacked on September 11 crashed in western Pennsylvania, killing all forty-five people on board. It is believed that the plane crashed after several passengers stormed the cockpit in an attempt to keep the terrorists from hitting their target.

DID YOU KNOW?

Pennsylvania is one of just four states that technically designates itself a commonwealth rather than a state. In the years between the Revolution and the ratification of the U.S. Constitution in 1787, "commonwealth" was a popular term for a state. This term was preferred by many political writers because it established the region more as an independent country than as a "colony" belonging to a central government.

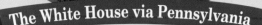

The White House via Pennsylvania

One Pennsylvanian has served as president of the United States.

JAMES BUCHANAN (1857–1861) was the only U.S. president from the Commonwealth of Pennsylvania. Buchanan was born in Mercersburg and educated at Dickinson College. He began his career as a lawyer in Lancaster and was elected to the Pennsylvania legislature in 1814. After terms as a U.S. Representative, U.S. Senator, U.S. minister to both Russia and England, and Secretary of State, Buchanan was elected the fifteenth president of the United States in 1856. Because he had been abroad during much of the bitter debate over abolition of slavery, Buchanan had not taken a public stand on the issue and was thus a "safe" candidate for the Democratic party, which opposed abolition. Buchanan served only one term. During his term in office, abolitionist John Brown led a failed raid on the U.S. armory at Harper's Ferry, Maryland. Brown hoped to use the weapons to incite a slave rebellion. The actions darkened the clouds of war over the nation and emphasized the fact that Buchanan's hands-off approach to the issue of slavery was not acceptable to either side. Buchanan has the distinction of being the only U.S. president who never married. He is buried in Lancaster.

Rural and suburban communities generally operate as townships. Most of these are called first-class townships, and they are governed by boards of at least five commissioners elected to four-year terms. Smaller townships, called second-class townships, are governed by boards of three supervisors elected to six-year terms. Pennsylvania's fifty-six cities, including Philadelphia and Pittsburgh, use the mayor-council form of government.

Pennsylvania is one of the few states that has a borough form of local government. These units of government are smaller than cities. Most of Pennsylvania's boroughs are governed by a mayor and by councils elected to four-year terms.

General Assembly			
House	**Number of Members**	**Length of Term**	**Term Limits**
Senate	50 senators	4 years	No more than 2 consecutive terms
House of Representatives	203 representatives	2 years	No more than 2 consecutive terms

A State of Graceful Aging

Home: the fields, red, with acid rows of corn and
sandstone corner-markers.
The undertone of insect hum, the birds too full to sing.
A Sunday haze in Pennsylvania.

— From "Leaving Church Early," a poem by John Updike

Pennsylvania is a state that does not hide its age. The Keystone State is proud of its long tradition and rich history. In fact, even as a youthful colony Pennsylvania was a beacon in the wilderness. For much of the 1700s, Philadelphia was a center of intellectual, cultural, and political life. By the time the Continental Congress met there in the 1770s, the City of Brotherly Love was known as "the Athens of America," a comparison to the ancient Greek center of learning. As Pennsylvania settlement expanded west, Pittsburgh became an industrial center driven by steel. The wealth generated by that industry helped fund museums, orchestras, libraries and universities. In the 400 miles (644 kilometers) between the major cities, the traditions exemplified in the music of Stephen Foster, the novels of John Updike, and the paintings of Andrew Wyeth were nourished. In many ways Pennsylvania has been as much a cultural keystone as a political keystone for the country.

▼ Robert Indiana of New Castle created this sculpture that stands in John F. Kennedy Plaza in Philadelphia.

Art and Literature

The man who seems to be in many places at once in U.S. history, Benjamin Franklin, was perhaps the nation's most celebrated writer during the mid-1700s. As the publisher of *Poor Richard's Almanac,* Franklin built a loyal following with his witty sayings such as "Early to bed and early to rise makes a man healthy, wealthy, and wise," and "Fish and visitors stink after three days." Even more important to the U.S. literary tradition, Franklin wrote the nation's first autobiography, and the rags-to-riches story of his life has become a model for countless autobiographies since. Other writers of Franklin's time included fiery political writer Thomas

▲ *Child in a Straw Hat* by Pennsylvania's Mary Cassatt. Painted circa 1886, it hangs today in the National Gallery of Art in Washington, D.C.

▲ Edgar Allan Poe

Paine. During the Revolution Paine wrote the pamphlets "Common Sense" and "The Crisis" in Philadelphia. In the mid-1800s, master of suspense Edgar Allan Poe worked in Philadelphia as a magazine editor. In fact, Poe wrote his first classic "locked-room" mystery, "The Murders in the Rue Morgue," while in Philadelphia. In modern times Pulitzer Prize-winning author John Updike of Shillington has written dozens of novels and essays. His best known character, Rabbit Angstrom, is a high-school basketball star who struggles through adult life in fictional Olinger, Pennsylvania.

Pennsylvania artists also have a long and proud tradition. The first Pennsylvania artist to achieve world fame was colonial painter Benjamin West, whose paintings of historical events are displayed in many museums today. Another famous colonial artist, Charles Wilson Peale, founded the

DID YOU KNOW?

Two of the nation's major symphony orchestras are based in Pennsylvania: the Philadelphia Orchestra and the Pittsburgh Symphony Orchestra.

Pennsylvania Academy of Fine Arts in Philadelphia, the first art college and museum in the United States.

Nineteenth century painters Mary Cassatt and Thomas Eakins are world renowned today, Cassatt for her Impressionistic works and Eakins for his realism. That realistic style passed on in the twentieth century to Pennsylvania painters N. C. Wyeth and his son Andrew. Another artistic family, the Calders of Philadelphia, are famous for sculpture. Alexander Milan Calder's giant statue of William Penn stands atop City Hall, and his grandson, Alexander Calder, gained renown for his free-form mobile sculptures, one of which hangs in the National Gallery of Art in Washington, D.C.

Museums

Not surprisingly, given the city's tradition, Philadelphia is also the home of one of the world's finest art museums, the Philadelphia Museum of Art. It is also the home of the Rodin Museum of sculpture. Across the state in Pittsburgh, the Carnegie Institute museum and library also exhibits many famous paintings.

The Thinker at the Rodin Museum in Philadelphia.

Lending Library

Philadelphia had the first subscription library in the American colonies. It was founded on July 1, 1731, by Benjamin Franklin and fellow members of the Junto. The Junto was a discussion group also known as the Leather Apron club. Those "friendly" discussions often led to disagreements, and the "Leather Apron-ers" needed to consult books for the right answer. At the time, however, few books were available because they were too expensive for most people to buy. Thus, by pooling their money, Franklin and his argumentative friends could afford a large library. Members of the library contributed money to buy books and could then use them without charge.

Fallingwater

Frank Lloyd Wright is considered by many people to be the greatest architect of the twentieth century. Although not a Pennsylvanian, he built what many admirers call his masterpiece in southwest Pennsylvania near Mill Run. Fallingwater was a summer home built for wealthy businessman Edgar Kaufmann in 1936. Wright's guiding concept was to create a structure that used much of what was already on the property — rock ledges, trees, and a rushing creek. The house is actually built over a waterfall. The American Institute of Architects has named Fallingwater America's most beautiful home. Fallingwater is now open to the public for tours.

Pennsylvania, in fact, is a museum lover's paradise. The Franklin Institute in Philadelphia is one of the finest science museums in the country. The William Penn Memorial Museum in Harrisburg and the Pennsylvania Farm Museum near Lancaster are both historical wonders. The Mercer Museum of the Bucks County Historical Society displays crafts and craftsmen's tools. Two important organizations, the Pennsylvania Historical and Museum Commission and the Philadelphia Historical Commission, oversee state and city historic locations and exhibits.

Outside of museums Pennsylvanians have also devoted a great deal of work to preserving traditional folk culture. The Amish, Mennonites, and other plain sects retain their customs and dress. In Lancaster County, where the Amish still farm with horses and oxen, horses and buggies are a familiar sight. The folk art and cooking of the Pennsylvania Dutch are also famous around the world.

Sports

Pennsylvania is ranked fifth in the nation in the number of major professional sports teams that make their home there. Baseball teams include the Philadelphia Phillies and the Pittsburgh Pirates; the Philadelphia 76ers are basketball giants; football fans can choose between the Philadelphia Eagles and the Pittsburgh Steelers; and hockey fans thrill to the Philadelphia Flyers and the Pittsburgh Penguins. Of even greater significance to Pennsylvania sports fans is that all of these teams have won championships in their respective sports.

Perhaps the most popular team in Pennsylvania, however, is the football team from Pennsylvania State University — the Nittany Lions — which has been one of the most successful teams in the history of college sports. On Saturdays in autumn the huge stadium at State College rocks with rabid Penn State fans cheering their team.

▼ The Pittsburgh Steelers play their first game at the newly built Heinz Field. The Steelers and baseball team the Pittsburgh Pirates formerly played at Three Rivers Stadium.

....
◀ **A chapel in Hickory Run State Park.**

Recreation

Pennsylvania ranks sixth among the states in tourism. Visitors are especially interested in the state's many historic sites. The state boasts fourteen sites administered by the National Park Service, including Independence National Historical Park in Philadelphia. Gettysburg National Military Park has set aside the battleground of the bloodiest battle in North America. Other military sites from the French and Indian War, the American Revolution, and the War of 1812 have been preserved or restored for tourists.

Lake Erie and the Pocono Mountains are popular vacation spots. Visitors to Lake Erie can enjoy summer water sports. Visitors to the Poconos can enjoy hunting, fishing, and skiing in the wintertime.

Sport	Team	Home
Baseball	Philadelphia Phillies	Veterans Stadium, Philadelphia
	Pittsburgh Pirates	PNC Park, Pittsburgh
Basketball	Philadelphia 76ers	First Union Center, Philadelphia
Football	Philadelphia Eagles	Veterans Stadium, Philadelphia
	Pittsburgh Steelers	Heinz Field, Pittsburgh
Hockey	Philadelphia Flyers	First Union Center, Philadelphia
	Pittsburgh Penguins	Mellon Arena, Pittsburgh
Soccer	Philadelphia Charge	Villanova Stadium, Villanova
Lacrosse	Philadelphia Wings	First Union Center, Philadelphia

DID YOU KNOW?

Whatever the sport, Pennsylvania's professional teams have always had a reputation as tough, gritty, winners. Their nicknames often go along with the reputation. When pro football's Pittsburgh Steelers won four Super Bowls in five years during the 1970s, their defense was known as "The Steel Curtain." During that same era pro hockey champions the Philadelphia Flyers were called "The Broad Street Bullies," after the street where the arena was located.

Keys to the Keystone

> You shall be governed by laws of your own making,
> and live a free, and if you will, a sober and industrious people."
> — *William Penn*

Following are only a few of the thousands of people who lived, died, or spent most of their lives in Pennsylvania and made extraordinary contributions to the state and the nation.

DANIEL BOONE
FRONTIERSMAN

BORN: *November 2, 1734, Berks County*
DIED: *September 26, 1820, St. Charles, MO*

Legendary frontiersman Daniel Boone was born in a log farmhouse east of Reading, Pennsylvania, the son of an English Quaker. When Boone was fifteen, his family moved west. Young Boone's name would become well known on the U.S. frontier as he helped settle the Kentucky wilderness. The Boones were among the first Europeans to settle there. Boone was among those who blazed the first trail through the rugged Cumberland Gap, a notch in the Appalachian Mountains near the point at which the borders of Virginia, Tennessee, and Kentucky meet.

LOUISA MAY ALCOTT
AUTHOR

BORN: *November 29, 1832, Germantown*
DIED: *March 6, 1888, Boston, MA*

During her lifetime Louisa May Alcott was a friend of established writers Ralph Waldo Emerson and Henry David Thoreau, yet her enduring fame came from her own writing. Fame was slow to arrive for the young author, however. Her first works, "penny dreadfuls," were the lurid tales she wrote while supporting herself as a teacher and a household servant. Alcott finally achieved fame with her autobiographical novel *Little Women* (1868), the story of sisters Meg, Jo, Beth, and Amy. Its sequels include *Little Men* (1871) and *Jo's Boys* (1886); her works are recognized today as classics of U.S. literature.

MARY CASSATT
ARTIST

BORN: *May 22, 1844, Allegheny City*
DIED: *June 14, 1926, Chateau de Beaufresne, near Paris, France*

Mary Cassatt was born in Allegheny City, today known as Pittsburgh. She studied art at the Pennsylvania Academy of Fine Arts in Philadelphia as a young woman. After completing her studies she traveled extensively in Europe, finally settling in Paris in 1874. That year one of her paintings was displayed at the famous Salon art gallery, and soon Cassatt met French painter Edgar Degas. She became close friends with the well-known Impressionist. Remaining in Paris, Cassatt followed the work of the French Impressionists — and was invited to start exhibiting with them. Impressionism is a style of painting that portrays the effects of natural light on objects. Her later work was also influenced by Japanese printmaking. Cassatt became an important supporter of the arts and was successful in promoting Impressionism and the Impressionist works.

NELLIE BLY
JOURNALIST

BORN: *May 5, 1867?, Cochran's Mills*
DIED: *January 27, 1922, New York, NY*

At the young age of eighteen, Elizabeth Cochrane became a newspaper reporter for the *Pittsburgh Dispatch*. The paper's editor gave her the pen name of Nellie Bly, taken from a famous song by fellow Pennsylvanian Stephen Foster. Bly later moved to New York City to work for the *New York World*, where she became journalism's first investigative reporter. For one story Bly pretended to be a thief in order to get arrested and observe the treatment of women prisoners. For another story she pretended to be insane to investigate the New York City Mental Hospital. That led to a grand jury investigation of the treatment of patients. In perhaps her most famous stunt, Bly outdid the hero of Jules Verne's novel *Around the World in Eighty Days*. Bly traveled the world in seventy-two days, sending back reports to eager readers as she traveled by steamship, railroad, horseback, and foot all the way around the world.

W. C. FIELDS
ACTOR

BORN: *January, 29, 1880, Philadelphia*
DIED: *December 25, 1946, Pasadena, CA*

W.C. Fields was one of the United States's best loved film stars and comedic entertainers. Born William Claude Dukenfield in Philadelphia, Fields ran away from home at age eleven. Three years later he entered show business, joining the vaudeville circuit as a comic juggler. Fields eventually began performing on Broadway, in New York City, at the Ziegfeld Follies and also began working in theater. In 1925 he made his first movie and eventually starred as Mr. Micawber in *David Copperfield* (1935) and in other films such as the wildly funny *My Little Chickadee* (1940).

RACHEL CARSON
WRITER, SCIENTIST, AND ECOLOGIST

BORN: *May 24, 1907, Springdale*
DIED: *April 14, 1964, Silver River, MD*

Rachel Louise Carson graduated from Pennsylvania College for Women (now Chatham College) in 1929, studied at the Woods Hole Marine Biological Laboratory, and received a graduate degree in zoology from Johns Hopkins in 1932. Her love for and knowledge about wildlife garnered her the position of aquatic biologist and, later, chief of publications for the U.S. Fish and Wildlife Service. While there she wrote her first prize-winning study of the ocean, *The Sea Around Us* (1952). The book made Carson famous as a science writer, and she decided to devote herself to writing full time. Ten years later she wrote her most famous book, *Silent Spring* (1962), in which she warned against the danger of pesticides in the environment. It was largely due to this book that the use of the pesticide DDT was banned in the United States. The book became a bestseller, and Carson became known as one of the first U.S. environmentalists.

JIMMY STEWART
ACTOR

BORN: *May 20, 1908, Indiana, PA*
DIED: *July 2, 1997, Beverly Hills, CA*

Hollywood legend James Stewart was born in Indiana, Pennsylvania. After graduating from Princeton, Stewart joined a theater company. By 1935 he had landed his first movie role in Hollywood and soon was on his way to a fifty-year career as one of America's most beloved actors. Stewart won an Oscar in 1940 for his role in *The*

Philadelphia Story, but he is probably best known for his role as George Bailey in Frank Capra's movie *It's A Wonderful Life* (above). Today, his hometown is the site of the Jimmy Stewart Museum.

FRED ROGERS
ENTERTAINER

BORN: *March 20, 1928, Latrobe*

The creator and star of the long-running *Mr. Rogers' Neighborhood*, Fred McFeely Rogers moved to Pittsburgh in 1953 to work at WQED, the nation's first community-supported public television station. His first television show, *The Children's Corner*, lasted for seven years and introduced many familiar "Neighborhood" characters, such as Daniel Striped Tiger, King Friday XIII, the Owl, and Lady Elaine Fairchilde.

While making *Children's Corner*, Rogers attended both the Pittsburgh

Theological Seminary and the University of Pittsburgh's Graduate School of Child Development. He was ordained as a Presbyterian minister in 1963 and chose to continue working with children and families through the media. In 1966 Rogers created *Mr. Rogers' Neighborhood.* Rogers has received numerous awards, and in 1999 he was inducted into the Television Hall of Fame. He finally retired in 2001; he and his wife live in Pittsburgh.

GRACE KELLY
ACTRESS AND PRINCESS

BORN: *November 12, 1929, Philadelphia*
DIED: *September 14, 1982, Monte Carlo, Monaco*

How many states can claim to be the birthplace of a princess? Grace Kelly was born in Philadelphia and attended Temple University. She left college to attend the American Academy of Dramatic Arts in New York City, making her Broadway debut in 1949. In her first major film role, Kelly starred with Gary Cooper in the classic western *High Noon* (1952). She also appeared in *Dial M for Murder* (1954), *Rear Window* (1954), and *To Catch a Thief* (1955). Her beauty caught the eye of the nation, the world, and, in particular, Prince Rainier of Monaco. They married in 1956, and Grace Kelly of Philadelphia became Her Serene Highness, Princess Grace of Monaco. A tragic auto accident took her life in 1982.

BILL COSBY
ACTOR AND COMEDIAN

BORN: *July 12, 1937, Philadelphia*

William Henry Cosby Jr. is an actor, comedian, and educator who has been successful in almost every medium — on stage, on television, in movies, and in books. Cosby is perhaps most famous for his two ground-breaking TV series. In the 1960s *I Spy* broke racial barriers by featuring Cosby as the first African-American co-star of a dramatic series. In the 1980s Cosby returned with his hit comedy, *The Cosby Show,* which Coretta Scott King described as "the most positive portrayal of black family life that has ever been broadcast." Cosby also developed the cartoon characters for *Fat Albert and the Cosby Kids;* Fat Albert, Dumb Donald, Weasel, and the others were based on friends from his childhood in Philadelphia.

ED BRADLEY
JOURNALIST

BORN: *June 22, 1941, Philadelphia*

While Bradley attended Pennsylvania's Cheyney State College, he worked as an unpaid disc jockey for a radio jazz show. The radio experience paid off — upon graduating, he became a reporter for a Philadelphia radio station, later joining a CBS-owned station in New York. He served as a CBS correspondent in Southeast Asia during the Vietnam War. In 1981 he joined the television news show *60 Minutes* after having served as CBS News White House Correspondent. He has received numerous awards for journalism, including the Robert F. Kennedy Journalism Award and eleven Emmy Awards.

Pennsylvania
History At-A-Glance

1608
Captain John Smith sails up the Susquehanna River from Jamestown, Virginia.

1609
Dutch explorer Henry Hudson sails into Delaware Bay.

1638
Swedish fur traders establish first European settlement north of present-day Philadelphia.

1655
Dutch seize Swedish settlements.

1664
British forces drive out Dutch; Duke of York's rule established in Delaware Bay area.

1682
William Penn sails up the Delaware River and lays out boundaries of the "City of Brotherly Love."

1682
General Assembly passes the Great Law, guaranteeing freedom of beliefs.

1685
Philadelphia becomes the capital of Pennsylvania.

1755
French and Indians defeat British in battle at Fort Duquesne on Monongahela River.

1759
Bituminous coal discovered near Pittsburgh.

1763
Pontiac War breaks out; ends in 1764. Charles Mason and Jeremiah Dixon begin surveying Pennsylvania–Maryland boundary.

1777–1778
Continental Army spends brutal winter camped at Valley Forge.

1600   **1700**   **1800**

1492
Christopher Columbus comes to the New World.

1607
Capt. John Smith and three ships land on Virginia coast and start first English settlement in New World — Jamestown.

1754–63
French and Indian War.

1773
Boston Tea Party.

1776
Declaration of Independence adopted July 4.

1777
Articles of Confederation adopted by Continental Congress.

1787
U.S. Constitution written.

1812–14
War of 1812.

United States
History At-A-Glance

1781
Pennsylvania passes first law in the United States abolishing slavery.

1787
Constitutional Convention meets in Philadelphia; drafts U.S. Constitution; Pennsylvania is second state to ratify it.

1790–1800
Philadelphia is the capital of the United States.

1812
State capital moved to Harrisburg.

1863
Battle of Gettysburg, a Union victory, becomes the turning point of the Civil War; Lincoln delivers Gettysburg Address in November.

1873
Andrew Carnegie begins large-scale iron and steel operations.

1889
Johnstown destroyed by flood; about 2,200 killed.

1902
One hundred fifty thousand coal miners strike in western Pennsylvania; President Theodore Roosevelt orders mine operators to negotiate with mine workers.

1971
Clean Air Act passed; coal industry affected.

1979
Accident at Three Mile Island nuclear power plant near Middletown releases radioactive gases.

1984
Congress honors William Penn and his wife, Hannah, by naming them honorary citizens of the United States.

2001
An airplane hijacked by terrorists crashes into farmland in western Pennsylvania.

1800   **1900**   **2000**

1848
Gold discovered in California draws eighty thousand prospectors in the 1849 Gold Rush.

1861–65
Civil War.

1869
Transcontinental Railroad is completed.

1917–18
U.S. involvement in World War I.

1929
Stock market crash ushers in Great Depression.

1941–45
U.S. involvement in World War II.

1950–53
U.S. fights in the Korean War.

1964–73
U.S. involvement in Vietnam War.

2000
George W. Bush wins the closest presidential election in history.

2001
A terrorist attack in which four hijacked airliners crash into New York City's World Trade Center, the Pentagon, and farmland in western Pennsylvania leaves thousands dead or injured.

▼ **Independence Square as it was on March 31, 1917.**

Festivals and Fun For All

Check Web site for exact date and directions.

Lehigh Valley Blues and Jazz Festival, Coplay

A great lineup of talented artists from around the country and around the corner.
www.lvbluesfest.com

Central Pennsylvania Festival of the Arts, State College

A nationally recognized sidewalk sale and exhibition, two juried gallery shows, and music, dance, and theatrical performances.
arts-festival.com

German Festival, Kutztown

The finest in traditional crafts, food, music, and folklife.
www.kutztownfestival.com

Renaissance Faire, Cornwall

Hundreds of colorfully costumed merrymakers recreate a sixteenth century country festival.
www.parenaissancefaire.com

Audubon Art & Craft Festival, Hawley

Crafts exhibitors and artists demonstrate their techniques and sell their unique and original work. Pottery, woodworking, fine glass work, woodcarving, leather carving, wheat weaving, and metal working are just a few of the crafts featured.
www.audubonfestival.com

Westmoreland Fair, Greensburg

A nine-day fair that attracts close to ten thousand people each day.
www.westmorelandfair.com

Fall Foliage Festival, Bedford

Browse and shop in over four hundred craft booths lining the streets and the square in Bedford and in Fort Bedford Park.
www.bedfordcounty.net/fall

Central Pennsylvania Mellon Jazz Festival, Harrisburg

Celebrate Father's Day weekend with some of the country's finest jazz musicians.
www.pajazz.org

Pennsylvania Shakespeare Festival, Center Valley

At least two fully staged Shakespeare plays as well as quality children's plays.
pashakespeare.org

....

▼ William Shakespeare.

▲ Reenactment of a Civil War battle.

Musikfest, **Bethlehem**

Musikfest is one of the largest U.S. music festivals, featuring more than one thousand free musical performances.

www.musikfest.org

Philadelphia Folk Festival, **Schwenksville**

A three-day extravaganza of traditional and contemporary folk music, dance, crafts, camping, campfire sings, storytelling, juggling, and special children's activities.

www.folkfest.org

Celebration of Women Writers, **Philadelphia**

The Celebration of Women Writers recognizes the contributions of women writers throughout history.

digital.library.upenn.edu/women

Pennsylvania Maple Festival, **Meyersdale**

Living history tours, a regiment of Union Soldiers, and live entertainment are all part of this celebration of the maple industry.

pamaplefestival.com/Index.htm

Pennsylvania Lottery Chocolate Festival, **Philadelphia**

Cooking demonstrations, make-and-take crafts, games, vendors, and free samples of various chocolate treats.

www.tall.org/clubs/pa/tcop/flyers/
pennlottchocfest.html

Philadelphia Fringe Festival, **Philadelphia**

Thought-provoking theater, dance, performance art, music, poetry, puppetry, and visual arts performed by national and international artists.

www.pafringe.com

Books

Bartoletti, Susan Campbell. *Growing Up in Coal Country.* New York: Houghton Mifflin, 1996. Children who worked in Pennsylvania coal mines one hundred years ago, and how they lived.

Gallagher, Jim. *The Johnstown Flood.* New York: Chelsea House, 2000. In 1889 a dam broke and drowned Johnstown, Pennsylvania, in one of the nation's worst floods.

Giblin, James and Michael Dooling. *The Amazing Life of Benjamin Franklin.* New York: Scholastic, 2000. The life of a fascinating man who was an inventor, printer, writer, and helped compose the U.S. Constitution.

Kroll, Steven and Ronald Himler. *William Penn: Founder of Pennsylvania.* New York: Holiday House, 2000. Learn more about the man who established the colony of Pennsylvania and the city of Philadelphia.

Murphy, Jim. *The Long Road to Gettysburg.* New York: Clarion Books, 2000. Find out more about the Battle of Gettysburg and its importance in the Civil War.

Wills, Charles A. *A Historical Album of Pennsylvania.* Brookfield, CT: Millbrook Press, 1996. Read more about Pennsylvania's interesting past.

Web Sites

▶ Official state site
www.state.pa.us/PAPower

▶ Official site of the city of Philadelphia
www.phila.gov

▶ Pennsylvania Historical Society
www.phmc.state.pa.us

Films

Hoyt, Austin. *The Richest Man in the World: Andrew Carnegie.* Boston, MA: American Experience/WGBH, 1997. The rags-to-riches story of a poor immigrant boy who built a fortune in railroads and steel, and then gave most of it away.

Gazit, Chana. *Meltdown at Three Mile Island.* Boston, MA: Steward/Gazit Productions, Inc./The American Experience/WGBH, 1999. The story behind the near-nuclear tragedy at a Pennsylvania power plant.

Note: Page numbers in *italics* refer to illustrations or photographs.

A

abolitionists, 13–14
Adams, John, 12
African-Americans, 13–14
age distribution, *16,* 17
agriculture, 21–22, 26–27
airports, 27
Alcott, Louisa May, 38
Algonquian Indians, 9
Allegheny Mountains, 22, 27
Allegheny River, 20, 23
Amish, 18, 19, *19,* 35
animals, 6, *20*
anthracite, *26*
Appalachian Highlands, 21
Appalachian Mountains, 14
Appalachian Plateau, 22
Appalachian Ridge and Valley
  Region, 22
architecture, *35*
area, 6
Argall, Samuel, 10
arts, 32, 33–34
Atlantic Coastal Plain, 23
attractions
  arts, 32, 33–34
  Daniel Boone
    Homestead, 7
  festivals, 44–45
  mountains, 20, 21, 22, 23
  museums, 34–35
  music, 33
  parks, 7, 23, 37
  rivers, 20, 23, 24
  sports, 17, 36–37
Audubon Art & Craft
  Festival, 44

B

Barry, John, *5*
baseball, 37
basketball, 37
Battle of Bushy Run, 12
Battle of Gettysburg, 13–14
Berks County, *20*
bird (state), 6
Blue Ridge Mountains, 23
Bly, Nellie, 39
books about Pennsylvania, 46
Boone, Daniel, 38
Bowman's Hill, *20*
Bradley, Ed, 41
Brethren, 19
Brown, John, 31
Buchanan, James, 13, 31
Buchanan Valley, 23
Bucks County, *20*

C

Calder, Alexander, 34
Calder, Alexander
  Milan, 34
cannons, *23*
capitals, 6, 13, 15, 28
capitol building, *29*
Carnegie, Andrew, 13
Carnegie Foundation, 13
Carnegie Institute, 34
Carnegie Steel Corp., 13
Carson, Rachel Louise, 40
Cassatt, Mary, 33, 34, 39
cattle industry, 26
Cayuga Indians, 9
Celebration of Women
  Writers, 45
Central Pennsylvania Festival
  of the Arts, 44
Central Pennsylvania Mellon
  Jazz Festival, 44
Charles II, 10
Charter of Pennsylvania, 10
Child in a Straw Hat
  (Cassatt), *33*
Children's Corner, 40–41
chocolate, 7
cities, 6
Civil War, 4, 13–14, *45*
Clean Air Act (1971), 25
climate, 21
coal, 4, 14, 25, *26*
"Common Sense" (Paine), 33
Commonwealth Court, 29–30
commonwealth status, 30
Continental Congress, 12
Cosby, William Henry, Jr., 41
courts, 29–30
"Crisis, The" (Paine), 33
Cumberland Gap, 38

D

dairy farming, 26
Daniel Boone Homestead, 7
Declaration of Independence,
  11, 13, 15, 28
Declaration of Independence
  (Trumbell), *9*
Degas, Edgar, 39
Delaware, 10
Delaware Bay, 10
Delaware Indians, 8
Delaware River, *18, 20,*
  23, 27
Delaware Water Gap, 22–23
Director of Homeland
  Security, 30
Dixon, Jeremiah, 12
dog (state), 6
Drake, Edwin, 14
Dunkers, 19

E

Eakins, Thomas, 34
economy
  agriculture, 21–22, 26–27
  coal, 4, 14, 25, *26*
  employers, 24
  gross state product, 25,
    25
  industry, 4, 13, 14, 24, 26, 32
  labor disputes, 15, 24
  manufacturing, 24
  railroads, 24
  resources, 25
  tourism, 37
education, *18,* 18–19, 36
employers, 24
environmental issues, 25
Erie Indians, 8
ethnic background, 17
executive branch, 29, 30–31
explorers, 10

F

Fall Foliage Festival, 44
Fallingwater, *35*
farm products, 27
festivals, 44–45
Fields, W. C., 39
films about Pennsylvania, 46
First Continental Congress,
  12, 15
First Frame of Government, 11
fish (state), 6
flower (state), 6
football, *36,* 37
fossil (state), 6
Foster, Stephen, 32
Franklin, Benjamin, *11,* 13, 16,
  19, 33, 34
Franklin Institute, 35
French and Indian War, 8–9, 11
Friends' Public School,
  The 19
fruit crops, 27

G

General Assembly, 11, 28,
  29, 31
geography, 20–23, *22*
German Festival, 44
German immigrants, 11
Gettysburg, *23*
Gettysburg Address, 7, 14
Gettysburg National Military
  Park, 37
Great Law, 4, 11
Great Railroad Strike, 15
Great Valley, 22
gross state product, 25, *25*
groundhog, *7*
Groundhog Day (film), 7

H

Harrisburg, 28, *29*
Harrisburg International
  Airport, 27
hedgehog, 7
Heinz Field, *36*
Henry, Patrick, 12
Hershey, 7
Hershey, Milton S., 7
Hickory Run State Park, *37*
Hispanic culture, 17
Historic Park, 7
hockey, 37
House of Representatives,
  29, 31
Hudson, Henry, 10

I

immigration, 11, 16, *16*
Independence Hall, *5, 7,* 12
Independence National
  Historical Park, 37
Independence Square, *42–43*
Indiana, Robert, 32
industry, 4, 13, 14, 24, 26, 32
insect (state), 6
Intolerable Acts, 12
iron industry, 14
Iroquois Confederacy, 8, 9

J

Jay, John, 12
Jefferson, Thomas, 13
John F. Kennedy Plaza, *32*
judicial branch, 29–30
Junto, 34

K

Kaufmann, Edgar, 35
KDKA radio, 34
Kelly, Grace, 41
Keystone State, 4
Kipling, Rudyard, 20

L

labor disputes, 15, 24
lacrosse, 37
Lake Conneaut, 23
Lake Erie, 37
lakes, 23
Lancaster, 28
Latino culture, 17
legislative branch, 28, 29
Lehigh River, 23
Lehigh Valley Blues and Jazz
  Festival, 44
Lehigh Valley International
  Airport, 27
Lenni Lenape Indians, 8, 10
Liberty Bell, 7
libraries, 34

limestone, 26
Lincoln, Abraham, 13
literature, 33–34
local government, 30–31

M
Mahican Indians, 8, 9
manufacturing, 24
maps of Pennsylvania, *5, 22, 25*
Martin Guitar Company, 27
Mason, Charles, 12
Mason-Dixon Line, 12
Mennonites, 19, 35
Mercer Museum, 35
Mr. Rogers Neighborhood, 40–41
Mohawk Indians, 9
Monongahela River, 20, 23, 27
Moravians, 19
motto (state), 6
Mount Davis, 22, 23
mountains, 20, 21, 22, 23
Murray, Bill, 7
museums, 34–35
music, 33, 45
Musikfest, 45

N
National Military Park, 23
national parks, 37
Native Americans of Pennsylvania, 8–9, 11–12, *12*
natural gas, 26
New England Uplands, 23
Nittany Lions, 36
nuclear power, 15, *15*

O
Ohio River, 20, 23, 27
oil industry, 14
Oneida Indians, 9
orchestras, 33

P
Paine, Thomas, 33
parks, 7, 23, 37
Peale, Charles Wilson, 33–34
Penn, William, 10–11, *12,* 28, 38
Pennsylvania Academy of Fine Arts, 34
Pennsylvania Dutch, 18, 19
Pennsylvania Emancipation Act, 13–14
Pennsylvania Farm Museum, 35
Pennsylvania Historical and Museum Commission, 35

Pennsylvania Lottery Chocolate Festival, 45
Pennsylvania Maple Festival, 45
Pennsylvania Railroad, 27
Pennsylvania Shakespeare Festival, 44
Pennsylvania State University, 36
Pennsylvania Turnpike, 27
Philadelphia, *18*
   as state capital, 28
   as U.S. capital, 28
   historical significance, 4, 12, 15
   inland waterways, 27
   named by Penn, 11
   size, 16, 18
Philadelphia Academy, 19
Philadelphia Eagles, 36
Philadelphia Flyers, 36, 37
Philadelphia Folk Festival, 45
Philadelphia Fringe Festival, 45
Philadelphia International Airport, 27
Philadelphia (Kipling), 20
Philadelphia Museum of Art, 34
Philadelphia Orchestra, 33
Philadelphia Phillies, 36
Philadelphia 76ers, 36
Piedmont region, 23
Pittsburgh, 16, 20, 27
Pittsburgh Dispatch, 39
Pittsburgh International Airport, 27
Pittsburgh Penguins, 36
Pittsburgh Pirates, 36
Pittsburgh Steelers, 36, *36,* 37
Pittsburgh Symphony Orchestra, 33
"Plain Sects," 18, 19
Pocono Mountains, *20,* 22, 23, 37
Poe, Edgar Allan, 33, *33*
politics and political figures
   Adams, John, 12
   Brown, John, 31
   Buchanan, James, 13, 31
   Charles II, 10
   Continental Congress, 32
   Declaration of Independence, 11, 13, 15, 28
   Franklin, Benjamin, *11,* 13, 16, 19, 33, 34
   Henry, Patrick, 12
   Jay, John, 12
   Jefferson, Thomas, 13
   Lincoln, Abraham, 13

   Paine, Thomas, 33
   Penn, William, 10–11, *12,* 28, 38
   presidents from Pennsylvania, *31*
   Ridge, Tom, 30
   Smith, John, 10
   Washington, George, 11, 12, 13
Pontiac's War, 12
Poor Richard's Almanac, 33
population, 6, 17
Porter, Robert, 14
ports, 20
presidents from Pennsylvania, *31*
Printz, Johan, 10
Pymatuning Reservoir, 23

Q
Quakers, 10, 18, 19

R
radio, 34
railroads, 24
rainfall, 21
Raystown Lake, 23
recreation, 37
religious makeup of Pennsylvania, 17–18, 19
Renaissance Fair, 44
resources, 25
Revolutionary War, 4, 8, 9
Ridge, Tom, 30
rivers, 20, 23, 24
Rodin, Auguste, 34
Rodin Museum, 34
Rogers, Fred, 40–41

S
Schlatter, Michael, 8
Schuykill River, 23
Scotch-Irish immigrants, 11
Sea Around Us, The (Carson), 40
seal of Pennsylvania, *28*
Second Continental Congress, 13, 15
Senate, 29, 31
service industry, 24
Shakespeare, William, *44*
Shawnee Indians, 8–9
Shippingport, Pennsylvania, 15
Silent Spring (Carson), 40
slavery, 11, 12, 13–14, 17
Smith, John, 10
snowfall, 21
soccer, 37
Society of Friends, 10

song (state), 6
sports, 17, 36–37
State Constitution, 19
statehood, 6
steel industry, 4, 13, 14, 24, 32
Stewart, Jimmy, 40, *40*
Still, William, 14
strikes, 15
Supreme Court, 29–30
Susquehanna River, *10,* 23
Susquehannock Indians, 8

T
temperature, 21
Thinker, The (Rodin), *34*
Three Mile Island, 15, *15*
Three Rivers Stadium, 36
timeline of Pennsylvania, *42–43*
Tinicum Island, 10
Titusville, 14
tourism. *See* attractions
trains, 10
transportation, 27
treaties, *12*
tree (state), 6
Trumbell, John, *9*

U
Underground Railroad, 14
United Mine Workers, 15
United Steelworkers of America, 15
University of Pennsylvania, 19
Updike, John, 32, 33
U.S. Constitution, 4, 7, 11, 13, 15, 28, 30
U.S. Steel Corp., 15

V
Valley Forge, *14*

W
Wanamaker, John, 24
Washington, George, 11, 12
web sites about Pennsylvania, 46
West, Benjamin, 33
West, Thomas, 10
Westmoreland Fair, 44
wildlife, *20*
William Penn Charter School, 19
William Penn Memorial Museum, 35
Woolworth, Frank, 24
Wright, Frank Lloyd, 35
Wyeth, Andrew, 32, 34
Wyeth, N. C., 34